AUDIE MURPHY

A Life from Beginning to End

Copyright © 2021 by Hourly History.

Table of Contents

Introduction

Born on June 20, 1925, celebrated actor and soldier Audie Leon Murphy began life in a worn-down, dilapidated home on the outskirts of Kingston, Texas. He was the son of Emmett and Josie Murphy, two poverty-stricken sharecroppers of Irish descent. As was typical for sharecroppers in those days, the Murphys lived in a run-down house on someone else's land. They were allowed to live on the property where they worked and were given a meager fee in exchange for their routine services.

Along with Audie, the Murphys had a long line of other children, but only nine of these would live long enough to become adults. Audie was the seventh child to be born, and it's said that by number seven, his parents were at such a loss for names that they simply named him after a neighbor who had aided Mrs. Murphy during her pregnancy.

It was a hardscrabble life that Audie was brought into, and from the very beginning, he had to fight for every crumb he could get. It's said that Mrs. Murphy took baby Audie with her into the fields while she picked cotton, practically as soon as he was born. By the time he was four years old, he was picking the crop right along with the rest of the family.

Although Audie's mother and even his siblings were said to be hardworking, it has been insinuated that his father Emmett was not quite so industrious. People who knew Emmett would later claim that he was more into gambling away his wages than earning an honest living. It was apparently this streak of wantonness that eventually led Emmett to abandon his family. Growing up without a father, young Audie learned rather quickly what it meant to be a man.

Chapter One

Orphaned at an Early Age

"I can't ever remember being young in my life."

—Audie Murphy

Audie Murphy had to learn to work at a young age. In fact, he did not enter school until he was nine years old and would drop out when he was barely in his teens with just an elementary school education.

Although young Audie is said to have liked school and made A's and B's in his classes, he was often a source of disruption among his peers. Audie himself would later admit that he was a hyper, temperamental kid who frequently found himself in trouble. As Audie himself would later recall, "I fought every day. I guess I was trying to prove that I was as good as any of them. I lived on the wrong side of the tracks."

Even as a child, Audie knew that he had been dealt a bad hand in life. He had just one pair of outgrown overalls to wear to school (earning him the nickname "Short-Breeches"), and he often showed up hungry without a packed lunch. So, at a young age, Murphy made up his mind to drop out in favor of earning a full-time wage picking cotton. For this back-breaking task, he earned approximately $1 a day.

Along with his work as a sharecropper, Audie also learned to hunt for his own food. This was a skill that Audie perfected early on, first by simply throwing rocks at small animals passing by, such as squirrels and rabbits, and then later, through the use of a makeshift slingshot. As primitive as his methodology was, he was apparently quite good at bagging small game, and it was through these efforts that he was often able to bring home a rabbit or two that could be butchered and cooked up into a stew.

Once he was a little older, Murphy began to use a proper hunting rifle, and with this weapon, his hunting ability increased dramatically. It's really no wonder Audie became an excellent marksman in the military, considering his early experience with rifles. It's said that he could shoot the smallest of targets with incredible precision from many yards away. Both his eyes and his ears had become finely honed instruments, and even when he couldn't see an animal, at times he could accurately shoot the critter just by hearing faint movement, such as the cracking of a twig.

The concept of someone in the United States hunting to get food for dinner is admittedly a rather alien one to most people today, but in the cash-strapped post-depression era, it wasn't that unusual—especially in rural Texan communities such as those that Audie grew up in.

It was through all of these efforts that, for a time, Audie, his mother, and his siblings managed to eke out a stable existence. By 1940, when Murphy was about 15 years old, he took on a farm job away from home. Here, he worked as a hired hand making $1.50 a day for a local farmer named Haney Lee. Audie liked working for the Lees, and during his time with the family, he almost considered them something akin to blood relatives.

Mr. Lee especially took on a fatherly role for the teenager, even going so far as to be the one who first taught Audie how to drive a car—a skill which even as early as 1940 had become a major rite of passage in a young man's life. Audie Murphy was just beginning to come into his own.

Sadly, tragedy would soon come young Murphy's way when his mother abruptly perished from a bad case of pneumonia coupled with endocarditis on May 23, 1941. On the day she passed, Audie was working near his mother's home, hoeing a backyard garden. He knew she was sick, but her passing apparently caught him completely off guard. He was in the midst of his gardening work when he was suddenly called into his mother's house by those who had been attending to her. They knew that her time was short, and as Audie hurried inside, it was made clear that now was the time to say his last goodbyes. She died shortly thereafter, passing away at just 49 years of age.

It was truly a devastating blow for Audie. With the loss of his mother and the absence of his father, the now-teenaged Audie Murphy found himself an orphan. Not only that, but he had also become the main breadwinner of his family. Murphy would later recall this heartbreaking episode, stating, "She died when I was sixteen. She had the most beautiful hair I've ever seen. It reached almost to the floor. She rarely talked, and always seemed to be searching for something.

What it was I don't know. We didn't discuss our feelings. But when she passed away, she took something of me with her. It seems I've been searching for it ever since."

Despite his grief, Murphy had to pick himself up by his bootstraps and find a way for him and his siblings to survive. For a time, he made money working odd jobs. But the meager money he made wasn't quite enough, and the youngest of the children—three of Audie's little brothers and sisters—were eventually shipped off to an orphanage. Audie, who was really just a kid himself, was at a complete loss as to what he could do. His meager education certainly wasn't going to allow him to go to college, and he didn't have much of any means to gain decent employment anywhere else.

As it turned out, world events would soon spiral out of control and bring this country boy from Texas an opportunity he never quite imagined he would have. For it was after Japan attacked Pearl Harbor in December of 1941 that Audie Murphy found himself seeking to join up with the U.S. Armed Forces.

Chapter Two

Shipped off to War

"I have to admit I love the damned Army. It was father, mother, brother to me for years. It made me somebody, gave me self-respect."

—Audie Murphy

Just about as soon as the United States declared war, Audie Murphy sought to get enlisted to fight overseas. For him, it was not only a patriotic duty but also a means to gain meaningful employment since he had no other way to make a decent income. The army would provide him a means to escape the drudgery of being a sharecropper and open the door for far greater opportunities than he otherwise would have had.

As eager as Murphy was to become an enlisted man, however, there was one small problem—he wasn't old enough. His application ended up being rejected outright due to the fact that he was still a minor. It was only when his sister managed to cook up a fake document, declaring him one year older than he actually was, that he was finally successfully admitted to the U.S. military the following year, on June 30, 1942.

Murphy was then sent off to begin his induction into the army at a place called Camp Wolters in Texas. Camp Wolters had been in use by the Texas National Guard since the 1920s before it was taken over by the U.S. Army in 1941 to serve as an infantry training center. During World War II and the rush to enlist troops, it had become one of many weigh stations, which at its highest occupancy is said to have held nearly 25,000 troops.

Upon Audie Murphy's arrival at Camp Wolters, he was given what was essentially a welcome packet, which among other things contained educational materials as to what kind of instruction they would receive as a soldier in the infantry. Murphy also received his first army-issued uniform, had his hair cut, and was issued a gun. He was also placed in his first fighting division—the fourth platoon of Company D.

Audie Murphy showed much promise early on, and during the course of his introductory training as an infantryman, he managed to gain the coveted Marksman Badge for his excellent handling of a gun. He was so good with a weapon, in fact, that his platoon corporal used him to teach some of his fellow troops who were struggling so that they could get a better handle of their weapon. Despite this, Murphy's commanding officers were initially unsure if the young man would be able to handle the rigors of war, seeing as his health was quite frail and he was only 5 foot 5 inches tall (166 centimeters) and weighed in at 112 pounds (51 kg). They figured that perhaps he would be better suited in an administrative position or as a cook. Murphy flat out refused, however, and managed to convince them to keep him in training to become a combat soldier.

After being given a brief leave to visit relatives back home, Murphy was then shipped off for further training in October of 1942, this time at Fort Meade in Maryland. Although not a whole lot is known of Murphy's time at Fort Meade, many stories have been passed down. One such story is the recollection of Murphy attending a carnival that had popped up near the base with his army buddies. Audie apparently engaged in a carnival game that required him to shoot at playing cards from a great distance away. He apparently succeeded at this challenge, but the frustrated proprietor of the shooting gallery refused to acknowledge it and furthermore refused to give him the prize he had won—a quick, cool $25 in cash.

Cash-strapped Audie Murphy, who felt he could use every dollar he could get, was quite upset over the ordeal and even told his commander about it. His commander apparently didn't like the shenanigans of the proprietor too much either and decided to pay him a visit. The commander apparently convinced the proprietor to give Audie his cash reward, but the man insisted that he never wanted to see Murphy around his shooting gallery again.

It was after his training at Fort Meade came to a close that Murphy was then transferred to New Jersey's Camp Kilmer on January 23, 1943. This would be his last stateside transfer before he would be sent for deployment abroad. He eventually left New Jersey on February 8 onboard a transport craft called the *Hawaiian Shipper*. Despite the name of the ship though, Audie Murphy wouldn't be going anywhere near Hawaii any time soon. Rather, he would be headed to the fabled city of Casablanca, in Morocco, which had become a landing point for Allied forces seeking to drive the Axis out of North Africa.

Casablanca had been part of French North Africa, but when the Nazis defeated France in 1940 and set up a puppet regime known as Vichy France, the actual French grip on the region was tenuous at best. After Allied forces received intelligence that many of the locals disaffected by the Vichy French that administered the region just might turn around and support them, it was decided to touch down in Casablanca. The city was ultimately taken by the Allies in what was known as Operation Torch, a military campaign waged from November of 1942 to May of 1943.

Audie Murphy himself arrived in Casablanca on February 20, 1943. Immediately after his ship came to port, Audie and his fellow soldiers were placed on a train and sent some 60 miles (100 kilometers) north to a town called Rabat, where the next leg of the operation was being mobilized. Murphy was given an assignation with the 1st Battalion, 15th Infantry Regiment, of the 3rd Infantry Division. Here, he was placed under the direction of a certain Major General Lucian Truscott. One of the first major duties that Audie Murphy was given was the role of being a platoon messenger. Soon after that, the promising young soldier received a promotion and was made private first class.

Rather than seeing combat in North Africa, Murphy was tasked with guarding prisoners of war and training for the coming invasion of Italy. But although he was itching to see some real action, Audie wasn't too disappointed since, in his own words, he "learned more in three months of training in Africa than I learned in six months in the States."

On July 10, 1943, Murphy's Infantry group finally departed from North Africa and made landfall on the Italian island of Sicily. This was all part of the largescale effort to gain a foothold in the Mediterranean and begin the long march to Rome. Italy was, of course, under the control of the Italian fascist Benito Mussolini at this time. Of the three Axis powers of Germany, Japan, and Italy, it was Mussolini's regime that was considered the weakest. Thus, Italy—which was sometimes called the "soft underbelly of Europe" by war planners—became the first target in the effort to wrest Europe from Axis' control.

For Audie Murphy, the trip across the Mediterranean Sea was a rough one since a severe storm had broken out over the waters, but the storm was also a blessing in disguise since it worked as good cover against German reconnaissance, which had been keeping close watch over the region. Once the fleet of U.S. transport craft came to shore, it seemed that they had managed to sneak up on the island undetected. Upon landfall, the craft cut all of their lights off. The American troops watched quietly as searchlights from Sicilian defenders scanned across the waters, trying to find any sign of intrusion. They failed to do so, and to the great rejoicing of the Audie and his fellow soldiers, the threat of a fierce firefight as soon as they stepped foot in Sicily never did materialize.

Murphy and his group of soldiers were able to completely secure their beachhead, which was in proximity of Licata, a town of some 35,000 people. It was relatively calm at first, but as Audie and his group pushed forward, the enemy began to fight back, and shots rang out through the air. This was initially a new experience for Audie. He had never been fired on like this before, but it soon became part of his normal routine. As Murphy himself later described it, "From various points came the rattle of small arms, but we soon got used to that."

Audie also had to get used to the casual nature of death in warfare. His first taste of this came when he and his company had briefly paused their march for a rest when a shell was suddenly lobbed their way. Murphy would never forget the sound of an artillery shell whizzing through the air. He would later describe how this distinct sound effect caused his very "scalp [to] start prickling."

It was shortly after hearing this awful sound that the shell hit the ground, exploded, and left one of his fellow soldiers dead, seemingly in an instant. Murphy would later recall how the sight had caused him to consider how easily one could lose their life. Seeing the slain soldier, Murphy pondered, "So it happens as easily as that?" One second his brother in arms was alive, joking and relaxing with the rest of the troupe, the next second, his body was twisted and sprawled on the ground dead in a heap of rubble.

Soon after that, Audie would be the one doing the killing. During the invasion of Sicily, he had been made an advance scout, who checked out the dangerous perimeters of landing zones. It seems that Murphy's first close-up experience of combat occurred while on one of these patrols. It's said that he came across a couple of Italian officers near the Sicilian town of Canicatti. The officers were trying to make a break for it when Audie opened fire on them, killing them both. Murphy was questioned about his actions by a commanding officer, who wondered why he would shoot people who were clearly running away. Audie's explanation was simple. "That's our job, isn't it?" he said. "They would have killed us if they'd had the chance."

The truth is, as soon as Audie saw them running, in the heat of the moment, his mind snapped back to his time shooting rabbits as a youth in Texas. It was his habit to shoot as soon as a rabbit took off, and this is exactly what he did to the two Italian officers. At any rate, as Audie Murphy said, he rationalized their deaths because he figured they would have killed him and his compatriots if he had let them live.

At least initially (the nightmares would come with time), Murphy didn't lose much sleep over his actions. He would later sum up the whole mentality he developed during combat as being along the lines of, "Now I have shed my first blood. I feel no qualms; no pride; no remorse. There is only a weary indifference that will follow me through the war."

Chapter Three

The Road to Rome

"I was scared before every battle. That old instinct of self-preservation is a pretty basic thing, but while the action was going on some part of my mind shut off and my training and discipline took over."

—Audie Murphy

After Audie Murphy landed in Sicily, the fighting was initially sporadic and light. It wasn't until his unit reached the Sicilian town of Campobello that they came under heavy fire. On July 13, 1943, the battle got particularly rough. Murphy and his group found themselves entirely pinned down, stuck clinging to the side of a hill, as bullets came down all around them.

Audie knew that if they didn't get up and move, they would soon be killed. It was with this realization that he managed to break through the paralysis. Despite the danger, he got up and started firing from the hip as he headed right toward the Italians who were trying to kill him. As he rushed toward his opponents, he also screamed for his compatriots to follow him, which—with the help of his inspirational example—they did.

It was after the fearlessness Murphy showed in breaking this bloody stalemate that he was given the promotion of corporal. Audie Murphy, who had often been underestimated due to his youth, short stature, and slight build, was now considered a force to be reckoned with, and his superior officers treated him accordingly.

The next major leg of the invasion of which Audie Murphy was a part was to seize Palermo, the capital city of Sicily. As U.S. troops made their way to the city, the most treacherous thing they faced was not enemy troops but rather muddy, poorly kept roads that turned what should have been a fast march into a slow and arduous slog. As Murphy himself later put it, the "drive to Palermo" was more aptly described as a "foot race."

Nevertheless, the troops struggled forward, covering some 30 miles (50 kilometers) a day. Murphy began to suffer health problems during this relentless push to Palermo, and at one point, he even had to stop by the side of the road and throw up. He was able to recover, but the very next day he passed out cold from sheer exhaustion. Because of this, he ended up in a military aid station and was administered medical treatment.

Murphy spent a full week under wraps before he was able to hook back up with the invasion force. By then, Palermo had already fallen, and the Allied troops were in a good position to begin plans for the inevitable invasion of Italy proper. This meant marching on nearby Messina, which would place U.S. troops right across from the tip of the Italian Peninsula.

At this point, the Americans were fighting Germans more than they were Italians. The Italians were known to give up fairly easily, and soon they rendered many prisoners of war for the U.S. to take care of. The Germans, however, were another story. Far from home, and mostly seasoned veterans, the German troops that the Allies encountered in Sicily were fierce and typically refused to give up, even when the odds were stacked against them.

It was a tough fight to take Messina, but finally, the last of the Germans pulled back, and the Americans were in control of the city by August 17, 1943. From here, Murphy and his fellow troops would make their way across the narrow body of water known as the Strait of Messina and on to southern Italy. This crossing would be made by U.S. troops that September.

Shortly after the Allies landed, however, the Italian government had already hashed out their surrender to Allied forces. In order to understand these developments, one must understand the political complexities that were afoot in Italy at the time. Italian fascist leader Benito Mussolini had already been deposed that summer. Overruled by the king of Italy (Italy was indeed a monarchy in those days), Prime Minister Mussolini had been given a vote of no confidence shortly after the failures in North Africa and Sicily and had been removed and replaced by Italian General Pietro Badoglio. Not only that, but Mussolini ended up being arrested and thrown behind bars.

Mussolini's ally—Adolf Hitler—was, needless to say, quite shocked by these developments. And so, the Italians, fearing an outright invasion of Germans, sought to placate Hitler by assuring him that they would continue the fight against the Americans under Badoglio. This was, however, just a bit of theater on the part of the Italian government. In reality, they had no desire to continue the war, and behind the scenes, the Italians were actively putting out feelers with the Americans to begin the process of surrender.

At any rate, upon landing, the Allied troops set up shop near the city of Salerno. Murphy would take part in a scouting party that ventured alongside Italy's Volturno River and ended up getting waylaid by a German machine gun nest. One soldier in his group was killed, but Murphy's quick action of tossing hand grenades, interspersed with steady shots from his own gun, managed to save the day, killing five Germans and preventing a complete massacre of his group. Soon thereafter, Audie took part in the assault on the so-called Volturno Line, in which his unit managed to fend off a German incursion, leaving three Germans dead and four Germans captured.

For his efforts, Audie Murphy was promoted to sergeant that December. This was then followed by another promotion, this time to staff sergeant, shortly after the new year in January of 1944. The Italian government in the meantime had reached their agreement to officially end hostilities on September 8, 1943. Yet even with the Italian leaders on board for peace, the fighting in Italy would continue.

As soon as the Germans got wind of what was happening, they poured down from the north and took over Rome. King Victor Emanuel was quickly evacuated and would take up shop in southern Italy, which would essentially become a protectorate of U.S. troops. Allied forces now had to take on the German-controlled northern half of Italy, bristling with German troops as well as the Italian fascists who still remained loyal to the cause of the Axis. Despite all of their gains, Audie Murphy and his fellow soldiers knew that the road to Rome would not be an easy one.

Chapter Four

Murphy's Medal of Honor

"Sometimes it takes more courage to get up and run than to stay. You either just do it or you don't. I got so scared the first day in combat I just decided to go along with it."

—Audie Murphy

Audie Murphy did not get to participate in some of the first battles in the Italian campaign due to his deteriorating health. Just as the Battle of Anzio centered around the Anzio beachhead was heating up, Murphy found himself in a hospital in the southern Italian city of Naples, being treated for a bad case of malaria. He wouldn't return to the field until January 29, 1944, just in time to take part in the First Battle of Cisterna. This massive onslaught, which occurred near the Italian town of Cisterna, turned into an abject failure for the Allies. The Germans put up a ferocious fight and would not back down.

Despite the overall failure of this Allied battle though, Audie Murphy stood head and shoulders above the rest when it came to serving with valor and distinction. He so impressed his superior officers that he was made a platoon sergeant for Company B's third platoon shortly after the battle. Murphy was then sent back to Anzio and would remain in place there over the next few months. The next major bit of action he saw occurred on March 2, when Murphy and his company engaged a German tank. Murphy charged at the tank and managed to blow it up by way of lobbing a few rifle grenades at the armored vehicle. It was this feat that managed to earn Audie the Bronze Star.

Yet although Murphy was a real sight to behold on the battlefield, he was still human, and his health kept right on dogging him. By March 13, he was back in a field hospital once again, suffering from a second bout of malaria. Murphy was soon back in the thick of things though, proving his worth on the battlefield. His efforts soon gained him yet another badge of distinction—the Combat Infantryman Badge— which he was awarded on May 8.

Murphy and his fellow soldiers would then go on to liberate Rome barely one month later, on June 4. It was shortly after this that the Allies shifted gears, solidified gains in Italy, and turned their attention to France. Murphy would take part in the invasion of southern France known as Operation Dragoon in August when he and his battalion made landfall at the so-called Yellow Beach in close proximity to the French town of Ramatuelle.

The first major bit of action that Murphy faced was when his squad was ambushed by a group of Germans. Audie took evasive action, engaged the Germans, and managed to kill two and wounded a third. The group then got drawn into another firefight when a couple of German troops left a safehouse and acted as if they were about to give up. This was just a ruse, and the Germans opened fire when Murphy's team approached. Enraged, Murphy charged the Germans and singlehandedly stormed the compound. With his gun blazing, Murphy killed six German troops, badly injured a couple of others, and bagged eleven prisoners of war. For these actions, Murphy was awarded the Distinguished Service Cross.

Shortly thereafter, Murphy and his battalion marched on the town of Montelimar, which was taken by the Allies on August 28. It was for actions he took in these engagements that Audie Murphy was later awarded the esteemed Presidential Unit Citation award, which is given for acts of extraordinary heroism in the face of the enemy.

Murphy's next medal would be none other than the Purple Heart, which he would receive in light of a bad injury to his foot by a mortar round, sustained on September 15. The injury would leave him with a distinctive scar that he would carry with him for the rest of his life. After a brief recovery, Murphy was out engaging the enemy once again the following month. On October 2, he would receive the Silver Star for taking out four Germans and wounding a few more, in the process of taking out a machine gun nest located along the Cleurie River, in Lorraine, France.

According to Murphy, the machine gunner barely missed cutting him down. As he later described, "The Germans spot me instantly. The gunner spins the tip of his weapon toward me. But the barrel catches in a limb, and the burst whizzes to my right." Murphy seized this rare opportunity by lobbing hand grenades at the machine gun nest. This was how he ended up killing those four Germans and putting the rest out of commission.

Just a few days later, Audie Murphy showed even more heroism during an engagement at the L'Omet quarry. Here, he and his unit killed 15 Germans and wounded 35. Due to all of his exploits, Murphy was promoted to the rank of second lieutenant and given Bronze Oak Leaf Cluster for his Silver Star. Murphy would nearly lose his life on October 26, however, when he was hit by an enemy sniper's bullet.

The sniper managed to hit him in the hip, but Murphy, with lightning-fast reflexes and his trademark perfect marksmanship, shot back at the sharpshooter and managed to put a bullet into his head. Murphy may have gotten the better of the sniper, but the injury he had received was a bad one, and soon, it became infected. He was taken to a local hospital where he would have gangrene surgically extracted from the wound. For this injury and his heroism, Audie Murphy would receive the coveted Bronze Oak Leaf Cluster to add to the Purple Heart he already had.

Murphy would then return to his battalion in January of 1945, just in time to take the town of Holtzwihr in north-eastern France. They faced stiff resistance, and at one point, German forces struck an M10 tank destroyer—an American light tank—with armor-piercing rounds designed to destroy larger tanks. After it was hit, the tank destroyer burst into flames, and the American troops evacuated from the burning vehicle. Murphy took the initiative and, while the tank was still on fire, hopped on board to commandeer its 50-caliber machine gun, which he used to decimate the German infantry as it approached. Murphy did this for the better part of an hour, singlehandedly pinning down the Germans, only abandoning his post when he was out of ammo. In all, 50 Germans lay dead as a result of Audie's deadly use of that machine gun. For this latest, incredible act of heroism, Audie Murphy was given the coveted Medal of Honor.

Murphy had demonstrated above and beyond his courage, bravery, and sheer tenacity, and on February 16, he was given yet another promotion—this time to first lieutenant. If there was ever any question as to whether Audie Murphy had served with, the hero status of this one-man war machine was now all but cemented in stone.

Chapter Five

Hollywood Success

"Acting is daydreaming. And I had daydreamed all of my life. It was the only way I could escape my environment."

—Audie Murphy

After all of his incredible deeds during the war, Murphy was ordered away from the front lines so that he could be a liaison officer at the Regimental Headquarters. Murphy would not get the chance to see combat again, and he was on an authorized leave of absence when he received news that Nazi Germany had surrendered to allied troops on May 7, 1945.

With the European theater of the war coming to a close, Audie Murphy had to decide what he was going to do with the rest of his life. For such a distinguished serviceman such as Murphy, many had naturally assumed that he would head off to West Point to become an officer. Murphy apparently dismissed this notion when it dawned on him that his meager education likely wouldn't be enough preparation to get him through the rigorous academic testing expected at West Point.

Instead, Audie Murphy was sent off to Fort Sam Houston in the United States, while it was determined what his next post might be. In the meantime, he was given 30 days' leave. During this time, he made several public appearances and was even given a few parades. He also appeared in an issue of *Life* magazine that July, which ran a story about Audie being the "most decorated soldier."

Murphy was eventually given an honorable discharge and was released from service on September 21, 1945. He would remain with the Texas National Guard on inactive duty all the way until 1966. Murphy had certainly served his country well and had won quite a bit of prestige, but it was that *Life* magazine piece that would put him on Hollywood's radar and introduce him to an even larger audience.

None other than the legendary actor and producer James Cagney had read the article and was intrigued by Audie Murphy's service. So much so that he contacted Murphy and had him come down to California to meet with him in person. Once in Hollywood, Murphy was given a contract to star in several action movies. They figured that Murphy had the raw charisma they were looking for in a leading man. At the same time, they also knew that this green actor had to hone his craft.

As such, they paid for Audie Murphy to take as many voice, dance, and acting classes as he could to make sure that he would become the next big star. Audie did all of this while being practically broke and renting a room at a gym for shelter. At least at first, his new life after the war certainly didn't seem all that promising. As Murphy would later acknowledge, "I came to Hollywood because I had no place else to go."

Nevertheless, despite all the time he put in, due to what was cited as "personal disagreement," Audie Murphy wasn't cast into any films by James Cagney. Instead, he became a free agent and began close work with the famed theatrical instructor Estelle Harman. With Estelle, Audie went back to the basics, working on classic, Shakespearean plays. Yet it wasn't until he met a seasoned screenwriter by the name of David McClure that Murphy really received his first big break.

It was under McClure's direction that Murphy wrote his epic memoir *To Hell and Back* about his experiences during the war. The book was released in 1949 and became an instant bestseller. It was on the strength of this book that Murphy was finally able to land acting roles. After playing a few walk-on parts here and there, he took on his first major production by taking a lead part in the movie *Bad Boy*.

The film, which depicted Murphy as a young delinquent, was a box office success and would lead to better things. It would, in fact, usher in a full, seven-year contract with Universal Studios. This was just the kind of big break that Audie Murphy was looking for. Universal was interested in casting Audie in western movies, and the first production they cast him in was an epic telling of the life of the gunslinger Billy the Kid. The film was called *The Kid from Texas*, and it was, of course, none other than the Texas native Audie Murphy who reprised the role of Billy the Kid.

It was a busy year for Audie, and before year's end, he started in yet another film, a western called *Sierra*, in which he acted alongside a promising young starlet by the name of Wanda Hendrix. Along with her ability to act and deliver good lines, Murphy fell in love with Wanda herself and ended up marrying her on February 8, 1949. Murphy and Wanda's love would not last, however, and they would be divorced by 1951. Wanda would later claim that Murphy was too controlling and that he insisted she quit her film career upon marrying him.

At any rate, just a few days after their divorce, Murphy moved on to his next flame, Pamela Opal Lee Archer, whom he married just a few days after his divorce and would have two sons with, James and Terry. Murphy would later recall that the first time he met Pamela, he "was a goner" and that all he had to do was look at Pam to feel wonderful. After getting married, the couple spent what was meant to be a quiet honeymoon in Texas, but it wasn't as laid back and uneventful as they thought it would be.

In the middle of the night, Murphy leaped up with a gun after spying a prowler at the window. It was only because of the pleas of his new bride that Murphy put the gun down. The crook ended up making a run for it, probably never realizing just how close to death he was. Pamela proved to be a good match for Murphy and was someone who was mentally and emotionally strong enough to deal with some of his more entrenched problems.

In the meantime, Audie was becoming more and more widely known in Hollywood. He went on to star in a succession of films, such as *Kansas Raiders*, *The Red Badge of Courage*, *The Unforgiven*, and *The Duel at Silver Creek*.

By this point, the Korean War had broken out, and Audie Murphy reaffirmed his commitment to the armed forces by signing on with the Texas National Guard. Noting the Cold War tensions that were building, during his training at Camp Mayberry in Austin, Texas, Murphy solemnly declared that he thought that perhaps World War III had already started.

After spending time drilling new recruits with the National Guard, Murphy returned to California. His book, *To Hell and Back*, had in the meantime been making the rounds. Big whigs in Hollywood were convinced that the book could make an epic film, so the plan came together to cast Murphy as himself in a movie based on the book.

Murphy's movie depiction of his time during World War II came out in 1955, about a decade after his service during the war had come to a close. Initially, Murphy was hesitant to play himself and actually requested another actor, Tony Curtis, to handle his parts for him. This was declined, however, and Murphy was indeed ultimately convinced to play his own part.

The film starts with a depiction of Murphy growing up in Texas and then flashes forward to his time in the military. This is different from the memoir, which doesn't cover his childhood much. But all in all, it's a fairly accurate depiction of what Murphy and his soldiers went through during their stint fighting in World War II. The gritty realism of the piece really connected with moviegoers too. The film was a box office smash hit, and it made Audie Murphy not only a millionaire but also far more famous than he already was. It was this epic film that made Audie Murphy a household name.

Chapter Six

The Western Star

"I guess that all those westerns on television killed the market, I seem to be the only one left. I'll keep making them till they get wise to me."

—Audie Murphy

By the time the 1955 film adaptation of *To Hell and Back* was released for the silver screen, Audie Murphy had become well known in American households. Audie himself was a great promoter and had frequently hobnobbed and hammed it up on special promotional cameos on TV programs used to ingratiate himself with the public. In the run-up to the release of *To Hell and Back*, he appeared on the game show *What's my Line?* as well as the variety shows *Colgate Comedy Hour* and *Toast of the Town*.

Riding high on the success of *To Hell and Back*, Murphy went on to star in the wild west drama *Walk the Proud Land*, which finished production the following year, in 1956. This story was a biographical piece about the famed Indian agent John Clum who had served as an intermediary between Apache tribes in the west and the U.S. government. The film deals with Clum's several attempts to broker peace between Apache and federal forces, and especially his dealings with the famed Apache legend Geronimo.

Playing the role of peacemaker did not suit Audie Murphy well, however, and movie-goers were disappointed to see their now-familiar action hero playing a non-violent part. This film was ultimately a failure at the box office and a personal setback for Murphy. After this disappointment, he briefly left the western genre and starred in a couple of pieces with modern-day settings.

In 1957, for example, he started in the comedy *Joe Butterfly*. Unfortunately, this film failed to gain traction, leaving Murphy once again back at the drawing board. Disillusioned, he returned to the role of a western sharpshooter in 1958, this time starring as a renegade bank robber named Joe Maybe in *Ride a Crooked Trail*. The following year, in 1959, he played the lead role in three more westerns: *The Wild and the Innocent*, *Cast a Long Shadow*, and *No Name on the Bullet*.

It was with *No Name on the Bullet* that Audie Murphy would finally receive the success that he craved.

In this film, Murphy plays a hired hitman named John Gant. His character is such a quick draw that he always gets his targets to pull a gun on him first. His lightning reflexes allow him to finish off his opponent even when they have a head start, and in the aftermath, since they drew first, he can claim it to be self-defense. The film presents an interesting twist on the western genre, with Murphy being a rather ambivalent anti-hero. This movie despite—or perhaps because of—its complex narrative, was a tremendous success.

It was with help from the proceeds of films like *No Name on the Bullet* that Audie Murphy went on to purchase an 800-acre ranch in California, where he would stick to his country roots, maintaining a full stable of horses on the land. Audie loved horses. He loved riding them, and in later years, he loved betting on them, developing quite a vice gambling on horse racing.

In the early 1960s, Murphy starred on a variety of television shows, such as *Startime* and *The Big Picture*. He then went on to do his own TV series—a production called *Whispering Smith*. On the show, Audie played the role of

Tom "Whispering" Smith, a gumshoe cop who tracked criminals in nineteenth-century era Colorado.

Murphy's next major film in the meantime was another western feature called *Bullet for a Badman*. This was then followed by *Arizona Raiders* in 1965 and *40 Guns to Apache Pass* in 1967. By all accounts, Murphy should have been a wealthy man at this point, but he had a bad habit that had a way of draining his resources. Some are addicted to drugs and alcohol, but Murphy, on the other hand, had an insatiable thirst for gambling. It was later recalled how he would often play dice and cards right on a movie set, gambling away hundreds of dollars at a time.

Unfortunately for Murphy, as much as he liked to gamble, it seems he lost much more often than he actually won. His friend John Huston later remarked that Murphy must have been the most unlucky gambler he had ever met. "Always unlucky," he said, "*always*. Not unskilled, just unlucky." Along with games of dice and cards, Audie was also a habitual gambler on horse races. It's said that he would bet as much as thousands of dollars at a time on horses he thought were absolute shoe-ins to win. But again, his luck was usually just not in it. He ended up losing a lot of money in those days, and by 1968, things were so bad that the Internal Revenue Service was knocking at his door looking for unpaid taxes he owed.

By this time, Murphy had also become vocal about the problems that plagued him since returning from the war. Due to all of the terrible loss of life he had witnessed, Audie, not surprisingly, suffered from PTSD. For him, it manifested itself through thrill-seeking (such as gambling), insomnia, nightmares, depression, and violent outbursts.

By the late 1960s, as the Vietnam War and the anti-war movement heated up, Murphy also found himself increasingly at odds with the popular thrust of society. Soldiers were no longer celebrated like they had been when he first came back from World War II. It was a tough reality for this war hero to face. And, it was even tougher for him to find roles that were pleasing enough to market to the masses. Audie Murphy had found himself down in a hole, and no matter how hard he tried to get out, he just kept slipping further into it. He felt like he was in quicksand, and soon an outright intervention would be in order.

Chapter Seven

Addiction and Arrests

"War robs you mentally and physically; it drains you. Things don't thrill you anymore. It's a struggle every day to find something interesting to do."

—Audie Murphy

As his career began to wind down in the late 1960s, Audie Murphy—despite all of his previous earnings at the box office—found himself strapped for cash, so much so that he declared bankruptcy in 1968. And, money wasn't his only problem. Along with his financial distress, Audie Murphy had become increasingly plagued by his own inner demons. Long troubled by nightmares and disturbed sleep, he had been prescribed sleeping pills to help him rest. Many of Murphy's nights involved taking sleeping pills and putting a handgun under his pillow, as that was the only way he was able to gain enough peace of mind to close his eyes at night.

On the road promoting some of his work, one of Audie's friends was shocked to witness one of these bad dreams. He was awakened in the middle of the night to find Murphy punching the walls of the hotel room. Murphy looked like he was in the middle of the fight of his life, yet he was not awake nor aware of what he was doing. He was actively acting out the terrible dreams he was having in real time. This was the reason why he turned to sleeping pills. Without the numbing effect of the sleeping pills, Audie's tortured mind would rehash some of the most terrible moments of the war.

Although he never quite admitted it, those around him would later vouch that Murphy was also haunted by guilt over the men he had killed during the war. On the surface, he always put on a brave face and claimed that he considered the men who had died at his hands just the common casualties of war—nothing more and nothing less. Yet his ex-wife Wanda Hendrix would beg to differ. She would later reveal that she had once caught her husband in tears, watching a news segment on German war orphans. According to her, he broke down and cried at the thought that some of those kids just might be orphans because of the German men he had killed during the war.

Despite the brave face he often put on, the truth is that Murphy had a lot of demons to deal with. For many years, his number one strategy was to not so much deal with them but to simply suppress them. This he did through numbing himself with the medication subscribed by his doctors. It was after years of depending on sleep aids, in particular, that Murphy realized that he had developed an unhealthy addiction to the drugs. He realized he had to do something to break the habit, so he locked himself up into a hotel room and quit cold turkey. The sheer tenacity of this veteran's willpower was demonstrated in the way that he was able to become clean. Holed up for a week in that lonesome hotel, he successfully navigated through the worst of his withdrawal symptoms and came out the better off for it.

Not only did he clean up his own act, but Audie also became a spokesperson for veterans who found themselves struggling to come to terms with life after their military service had come to an end. He made efforts to counsel Korean and Vietnam veterans in particular and petitioned the U.S. government to do more for these veterans as well. Back in those days, the Department of Veteran Affairs didn't put as much emphasis on mental health as they do now. As such, typically only physical ailments were taken into account.

Audie Murphy, on the other hand, was an early advocate for a more holistic approach when it came to taking care of veterans. In consideration of the very little help out there at the time for veterans seeking to readjust to civilian life, Audie once famously quipped, "Our war dogs were detrained after the war—but not the soldiers." It was these efforts that would eventually lead to Congress passing legislation in 1971 that would allow for the posthumous establishment of the Audie L. Murphy Memorial VA Hospital dedicated to the treatment of veterans—body, mind, and soul.

For a time, it seemed that Murphy had really cleaned up his act and was ready to make his big comeback. His return to stardom would be sidelined in May of 1970, however, when he was arrested for assault and battery in Burbank, California. The incident apparently occurred after Audie confronted a dog trainer named David Gofstein, who had been looking after the dog of a friend of his. Murphy confronted Gofstein about an issue with the payment, words were exchanged, and the situation got heated. A fight broke out, and at some point, Murphy reportedly went so far as to pull out his gun and fire it into the air.

Mr. Gofstein no doubt felt threatened, and the police were called. Although Audie Murphy was taken down to the station and initially charged, he was later cleared of all charges. Audie was lucky, but his future prospects seemed to be running on fumes. This wasn't even the first time that he had been accused of assaulting civilians. In fact, there was an earlier incident in which he had what one today might call a bad episode of road rage.

Murphy was supposedly irked when he saw a couple of guys driving too close to some scooter riders in traffic. He yelled at them, and then they took it upon themselves to try and attack him. It didn't work. Taking on two guys at one time was nothing for Audie Murphy, and these two would-be assailants ended up in the hospital for their transgression.

At any rate, after this latest aberration in his mostly civil life, Audie Murphy was once again back on track to resume his career. He had by this point become a director of a company called Telestar Leisure Investments, as well as his own production outfit called FIPCO (First International Planning-Co). This film production company had just finished up production on a film called *A Time for Dying*.

At this juncture, Audie Murphy's life was most certainly starting to look up. Unfortunately for him, he just wouldn't have much more life left to live.

Chapter Eight

The Fatal Plane Crash

"In life, quality is what counts, not quantity."

—Audie Murphy

One of the strangest yet often least mentioned circumstances that were in play in the leadup to Audie Murphy's death was his relationship with the notorious Teamster boss Jimmy Hoffa. It's been said that Murphy himself was privy to confidential information in regard to one of the prosecution's witnesses that had been used against Hoffa. He had allegedly been tipped off that the tale that this supposed Teamster whistleblower told was false. If true, such information would have potentially helped Jimmy Hoffa during his trial. And, while it may be a bit of a stretch to insinuate that Audie's death occurred as a result, the fact that Audie died shortly after delving into these matters does tend to raise some eyebrows.

At any rate, it was on the morning of May 28, 1971, that Audie Murphy got on board a twin-engine Aero-Commander private plane and departed from an airport in Atlanta, Georgia. He was on his way to check out a manufacturer of modular buildings in Virginia, which his company Telestar was considering making investments in. With him were four other passengers.

During the flight, the plane had to divert toward the mountains due to bad weather and heavy fog. This would prove to be a fateful—and fatal—decision. The plane ended up crashing into Brushy Mountain in the Jefferson National Forest, about 12 miles northwest of Roanoke, Virginia. The plane is said to have exploded into pieces as soon as it hit the mountain. When the plane was finally discovered three days after the crash, the human remains were nearly unrecognizable, but Murphy's body was eventually recognized due to the distinctive scar on his leg caused by the German sniper who had struck him during the war. He was only 45 years old.

Murphy's body was delivered to Los Angeles, where his funeral was held on June 4, 1971. He was just one month short of turning 46 years old at the time that he died. It's said that hundreds of attendees were present for his memorial service, and even while this service was going on, another memorial was being held simultaneously in Murphy's native Texas. Flags all throughout the state of Texas were at half-staff for the next three days, out of respect for their most distinguished son.

Shortly after the funeral, Murphy's body was sent off to Arlington National Cemetery, where he was buried with full military honors.

Conclusion

Audie Murphy was, no doubt, a war hero. He was such a spectacular war hero, in fact, that such a basic statement as this almost seems to diminish how incredible he really was. Murphy had seemingly no fear of death, and in the face of danger, he was much more likely to charge forward than to turn the other direction. It's a rare character indeed, who could jump on top of a burning tank destroyer, man its 50-caliber machine gun, and singlehandedly keep a whole battalion of enemy troops at bay.

Audie Murphy undoubtedly saved many lives that day, but the fact that he killed so many Germans during the war wasn't exactly a source of pride for him as it was an acknowledged necessity. Murphy did not revel in the fact that he had killed other men; in fact, like many other soldiers, it came to haunt him for the rest of his life.

Nevertheless, Audie Murphy fought just as hard after the war as he had done on the battlefield to make the best of the time he had left in life. During his later years, along with all of his appearances in films and TV shows, he cameoed as a real-life champion for veterans' rights. He took on a leading role in the early fight to have the mental and emotional well-being of veterans like himself looked after. It is for these reasons and more that Audie Murphy will remain a hero and a role model for people across the world.

Bibliography

Evans, Art (2020). *World War II Veterans in Hollywood.*

Graham, Don (1989). *No Name on the Bullet: A Biography of Audie Murphy.*

Moldea, Dan (1978). *The Hoffa Wars: The Rise and Fall of Jimmy Hoffa.*

Murphy, Audie (1949). *To Hell and Back.*

Smith, David A. (2015). *The Price of Valor: The Life of Audie Murphy, America's Most Decorated Hero of World War II.*

Los Angeles Herald Examiner. (October 16, 1970). "Murphy's Assault Case Goes to Jury."

Abramski, Pvt. First Class Anthony V. (February 27, 1945). "Statement describing Murphy's 26 January 1945 actions at Holtzwihr." Accessed from https://catalog.archives.gov/id/299775

Hollen, Staff Sergeant Norman (December 1944). "Statement describing Murphy's August 15, 1944 actions near Ramatuelle, France." Accessed from https://catalog.archives.gov/id/299779

Ware, Kenneth L. (April 18, 1945). "Statement describing Murphy's January 26, 1945 actions at Holtzwihr." Accessed from https://catalog.archives.gov/id/299784

Weispfenning, First Lieutenant Walter W. (April 18, 1945). "Statement describing Murphy's January 26, 1945 actions at Holtzwihr." Accessed from https://catalog.archives.gov/id/299785

Printed in Great Britain
by Amazon